The Rebellion of Fear

The Rebellion of Fear

BAHA BURHAN

Order this book online at www.trafford.com
or email orders@trafford.com

Most Trafford titles are also available at major online book retailers.

Printed in the United States of America.

ISBN: 978-1-4269-5617-1 (sc)
ISBN: 978-1-4269-5618-8 (hc)
ISBN: 978-1-4269-5619-5 (e)

Library of Congress Control Number: 2011901034

Trafford rev. 01/21/2011

 www.trafford.com

North America & international
toll-free: 1 888 232 4444 (USA & Canada)
phone: 250 383 6864 ♦ fax: 812 355 4082

To my brother:
Abdullah

We get slaked from a glass,
one half empty and the other is filled by the air.

We have even come to a point where we dread not only to understand, but lest our understanding should be true. This fear drives us into perpetual hesitation in deciding so many things that have a very strong impact upon our lives. Thus, we start creating margins to resort to, out of our skepticism and hesitation, as if our confidence in the mind's ability to select were unreliable for adopting clear-cut boundaries and taking decisive attitudes. Thus, we remain captives of persistent fear, which has created in us a shaky horizon and immense hesitation. It has for so long driven us into diseases rampant in our souls, which are already exhausted by our current state of affairs. We would later on be obliged to do away with that deep-rooted fear in our memory.

As for the houses, they live a recurrent heritage and a memory of which they could never get out or even specify their stance about. Scattered houses here and there linked by narrow roads. Every house stands as a separate world with all the secrets of understanding and certainty and the deeply buried memory of rejection and skepticism. However, they are all linked with that road, which has always brought them together into one mass that is marked by the particularity of anarchy but the pretence of organization.

As fast as an escapee from death to life, we regain our consciousness, to realize that we are escapees from life to death; thereupon, we lose our consciousness again.

At the back of every ostensible loyalty,
a hidden rebellion lies.

*   *   *

Not in the sin as such,
the problem is when disclosed.

*   *   *

For a just cause, we think we live;
all fear is that we die for a lost one.

*   *   *

If defeat begets determination,
what have we left for triumph?

*   *   *

One spends one's lifetime
in search of the things one stumbles over.

*   *   *

Any better place than a sin
to hide in?

*   *   *

From others' experiences,
we learned that they hadn't.

*   *   *

In the dark, we look for the right way without
conceding in public that we are in the wrong one.

*   *   *

His eyeballs shiver upward,
as if blind from above.

*   *   *

Small things change us;
as for big ones, we do.

*   *   *

How strange that logic adopts its crisis,
without considering it part of it!

*   *   *

Any better thing than self-control
to know what suffocation means?

*   *   *

When thought depends on fear,
understanding goes in vain.

*   *   *

Just asking who the winner is,
is a loss to all of us.

*   *   *

The more we fear an idea,
the more we resort to it.

*   *   *

To the extent that accepting something
has been based upon rejecting it.

*   *   *

The battle always goes on high gear
on a narrow spot of a wide field.

*   *   *

The smart part in adopting the idea of abolishing any
threat, whatsoever, stands behind the continuity
of any power, whatsoever.

*   *   *

Once others want us to understand
means that they haven't yet.

*   *   *

There's a trick played by the soul,
to accept that which the mind rejects.

*   *   *

In the end, we have to choose; once done,
prisoners of our choice we become.

*   *   *

The bigger mind gets in what it holds;
the wider craziness gets in what it accepts.

*   *   *

On two we fly to achieve something high;
once done, on one we run.

*   *   *

Unwise is he whose wisdom
is the source of his depression.

*   *   *

Things we do express, hard-to-deny fears,
but we may claim that we deny.

*   *   *

What a life we spend looking for more details
to believe more the things we lie about.

*   *   *

The ability of the mind to convince itself in what is unjust
is bigger than its ability to accept the just.

*   *   *

Baha Burhan

We always play to win;
I wonder when we play to lose!

*   *   *

We confront major conspiracies against us
with minor ones between us.

*   *   *

It waits the whole night up;
when losing hope that we shall wake up, it rises!
What a sun, never bored of rising.

*   *   *

Between two uproarious sounds,
only silence deserves to be listened to.

*   *   *

We know there is something somewhere,
how strange that we insist upon
looking for them elsewhere.

*   *   *

Despite being professional in shedding tears,
we haven't learnt how to cry.

*   *   *

How could a sacred thought
live in a polluted river?

*   *   *

My memory betrayed me once;
thenceforth, I haven't stopped betraying it.

*   *   *

Too hot, no shelter,
we lie beneath our own shadow.

*   *   *

Our ability to create justifications of adapting to our
disability is larger than our ability to overcome it.

*   *   *

Bliss …!
When we forget that we are miserable.

*   *   *

The tragedy of our memory
is that we are its vessel.

*   *   *

We think that things are easy to understand,
to fall in the illusion of understanding them.

*   *   *

How could a Man defend himself when
accused of his innocence and sentenced to sin?

*   *   *

Is being unaware of what we want a problem?
Or does the problem lie in being aware of what we want?

*   *   *

Of the same reason it's hard to die twice, rather many times
of many reasons. What an experience we gain!

*   *   *

Just having different conceptions about virtue
pushes us to vice.

*   *   *

From inside a conflict, it's never easy for us
to convince ourselves that we are out.

*   *   *

Man is most oppressive to himself, when creating
a hypothetical foe he dedicates his life to face.

*   *   *

While sitting in the zone of craziness,
the easiest thing we do is to evaluate the role of mind.

*   *   *

Memory without consciousness,
or consciousness without memory?

*   *   *

There is always something
between what we do and what we believe in.

*　　*　　*

Without going unconscious,
how does one create another consciousness?

*　　*　　*

After defeat, just staying alive
is considered a great victory.

*　　*　　*

He who is part of his memory
isn't like he whose memory is part of him.

*   *   *

When we live our past every minute of our present,
our future shall be nothing but our past.

*   *   *

Absentmindedness is the only moments
during which we feel free.

*   *   *

What most feeds persisting in sinning
is that only the sinless pay for the sin.

*   *   *

The concept of right
has always been an abstract symbol.

*   *   *

It's too high a pride for the fire,
that it delighted Nero.

*   *   *

On the chessboard,
the utmost ambition of the pawn is to queen.

*   *   *

When logic gets into things,
they lose their disposition.

*   *   *

Even the notion of freedom
never addressed our needs.

*   *   *

When unable to do something,
we don't.

*   *   *

How come that we consider our disability strength pushing
us to another disability we consider strength?

*   *   *

It's the will of God …
that we forget what we have to do.

*   *   *

When history moves on,
morality is pinned unable.

*   *   *

"Thes" or "This" what's the big deal?
So long as they both refer to the same thing.

*   *   *

The nature of our understanding
is another face of the size of our anxiety.

*   *   *

On the pavements of needs,
even the sole-sized space could be sold.

*   *   *

What most tortures us
is our certainty.

*   *   *

The only goal that we don't want to achieve
is death.

*   *   *

Democracy of the word has always sought refuge
in the dictatorship of the idea.

*   *   *

Intoxicated by victory,
we forget to count our losses.

*   *   *

Man's destiny is that his sacrifice is
in as much as being away from the position of power.

*   *   *

Is it an option
to belong somewhere?

*   *   *

The godlier,
the weaker

*   *   *

Are we all in the right?
Or we are all in the wrong!

*   *   *

We buy fear for our hope
and sell certainty for our doubts.

*   *   *

Coming to cure
vindicates our failure in prevention.

*   *   *

He wants to be honored sacrificing himself,
but the rules of the game never allow the king
on the chessboard to do so. What a deplorable life!

*   *   *

All fear …
if snow melts away.

*　　*　　*

It seems we are heading to create a god …
to worship us.

*　　*　　*

We don't have to count much on logic
that is led by its crises.

*　　*　　*

We more disagree on our role
than we agree on our existence.

*   *   *

Ambition …!
Another face of hard-heartedness.

*   *   *

It is okay to disagree on the details of the vestment,
so long as the terms of reference are the same
when unclothed in the open.

*   *   *

The only tragedy death lives
is that it has to live on everything life expels.

*　　*　　*

Poor us when we do good;
don't we know that that makes more evil of them?

*　　*　　*

No worth of the victims
who fall in marginal wars.

*　　*　　*

What most delights Man
is the sound of his heels.

*   *   *

only our doubt isn't
subjected to our doubt.

*   *   *

Swimming to survive,
we learn how to drown.

*   *   *

The things that we most gather around
are those we dispute over.

*   *   *

Philosophy …!
An attempt to show harmony as if it were contradiction.

*   *   *

The most complicated things
are governed by the simplest ones.

*   *   *

When hiding behind our relative understanding,
each of us claims to be in the right;
who on earth is in the wrong?

*   *   *

We are keen to maintain death alive among us,
for it'll be our only shelter when life kicks us out.

*   *   *

Life is deals, some on the table and some under,
but they are all losing bargains.

*   *   *

The fertility of land made them worship it,
how strange that they used to
tread it each footstep.

*   *   *

Assuming a postulate to agree upon
made the dispute incurable.

*   *   *

On the chessboard,
no matter how they change,
the pieces' roles remain the same.

*   *   *

Looking at the stars,
we fear lest they should fall in our hands;
at what shall we look then?

*   *   *

The narrower the spot of doubt grows,
the more confused the concept of faith gets.

*   *   *

Same life,
same views.

*   *   *

The most truthful moments we live
are those during which we can't lie.

*   *   *

So much is done
when nothing is done.

*   *   *

To preserve our position as victims,
we make executioners of ourselves.

*   *   *

The deadliest still
are the things we most defend.

*   *   *

Getting rid of doubt burdens us with responsibility
we are unable to shoulder.

*   *   *

What is the point of reading correctly a wrong reality?
As long as we are always part of it.

*   *   *

If what is based on wrong is considered wrong,
then was it a sin that which on sin was based?

*　*　*

We don't have to look at truth
so long as we aren't prepared to live in darkness.

*　*　*

Being a foe of what he ignores
doesn't mean that Man is a friend of what he knows.

*　*　*

It is logical to reform corruption;
when not reformed, it will be illogical to follow logic.

*   *   *

To be in the heart of power might protect him;
to make it in his heart may destroy Man.

*   *   *

Even the reformative ideas clash against each other,
launching from a hostile background.

*   *   *

From darkness, we might see light and know its details, but
from light, how could we see and know
the details of darkness?

*   *   *

Ranging between the logic of reform and reforming the
logic, the reformative thought has been but barren.

*   *   *

Believing his own lies once
is enough for Man to acquire immunity.

*   *   *

The more the road slopes upward, the more bent we get, for
the bend to remain on a par with the slope.

*   *   *

What value has the mind got
if unable to protect its craziness?

*   *   *

We create hope out of an embryo living a pitch-black
darkness in a tight womb.

*   *   *

How could the reformative thought work in a willpower
whereby everything is dedicated for its survival?

*   *   *

Only the weak adopt the idea of good,
but as for the strong, they perform it.

*   *   *

What's the point so long as both
the loser and the winner kings stay on the chessboard?

*   *   *

It's a comfortable feeling to enter a war;
you in advance know you are the loser.

*   *   *

Our remorse …!
As big as our wishes.

*   *   *

Just to start a game is an implied confession
that we never accept the idea of equality.

*   *   *

Our dazzling success in understanding the logic of the crisis
might be an implied confession of our disability
to understand the crisis of the logic.

*   *   *

Blocking up the road before the reformative thought
is a step to rehabilitate the logical thought.

*   *   *

We move forward to the blessing,
but how could we abandon a curse,
without which we would never have been here.

*   *   *

The reasons we don't perceive
have always been stronger than
those we claim to perceive.

*   *   *

Kings play together with kings;
when necessary, they make them puppets.

*   *   *

The only thing we got from our losses
is our ability to claim victory.

*   *   *

Getting to the edge requires high eligibility for practicing
rejection, not mere rejecting.

* * *

When surrendering, we find ourselves forced
to sign an accord most of whose articles are ambiguous.

* * *

Isn't it enough for the reformative thought
to remain as a moral choice?

* * *

We wait too much,
as if the end in the things were the right form.

*   *   *

We count on logic to prove something,
to end up proving it counting on illogic.

*   *   *

Between our awareness and our death,
the only thing we harvest is a wait.

*   *   *

It is futile to search in the bottom
for things that float on the surface.

* * *

When we triumph, is it really we who triumph?
Or we be allowed to triumph?

* * *

We might know "how,"
but can we know "why"?

* * *

Baha Burhan

How could a logical thought consent to compromises
in the need-to-be decisive issues?

*   *   *

Only faith is able to contain the disability
we try to jump over.

*   *   *

No need to build roads
so long as communication is through tunnels.

*   *   *

Although he has what the black king does on the
chessboard, the white king takes a move,
perhaps out of his boredom,
trespassing on the properties of the black king.

*　　*　　*

So long as there is a chance
for coming back to square one, it means we did nothing.

*　　*　　*

It is possible for an individual to believe his own lies, but
how could a group of people do that?

*　　*　　*

The most panic moments of fear
are when we refuse to accept the logical results.

*   *   *

We believe that God is absolute.
Yet, we make intentions of Him and interfere in them.

*   *   *

The two kings stand a moment of mourning
for the victims, waiting for another one to come.

*   *   *

What significance is it knowing what we believe in
without recognizing its value?

*   *   *

Thought could not but go in conformity with what
the heart adopts. Or else, it falls in forbiddance.

*   *   *

Nothing more pleasant than an illusory moment
of success, whereby we redeem our actual losses.

*   *   *

We are not as we are as a result of an address,
nor are we going to change on account of a call.

*　　*　　*

To claim that we are distinguished by having mind doesn't
mean that mind is distinguished in its own entity.

*　　*　　*

We can't be an outcome of a plan
we set in the past.

*　　*　　*

There is a predetermined rejection for any reading
of history that doesn't go in conformity with
the sacredness of understanding it.

* * *

We are only strong-willed,
when insisting to accept what we don't understand.

* * *

We live the adolescence of life; we haven't come of age yet,
and that doesn't seem to be imminent.

* * *

The price we pay to survive
is higher than the value of our existence and survival.

*   *   *

Thought has to protect us from our consciousness,
not to let us into the mazes of a memory
that rejects this consciousness.

*   *   *

We cover our loins with a mulberry leaf reading:
"Here is the scandal."

*   *   *

The smart one is he who fears that which he doesn't know;
while the genius is he who fears that which he knows,
and they both have a bit of …!

*   *   *

A world … half filled with our doubts,
while our fears fill the other.

*   *   *

To fortify the idea,
we set up invulnerable walls but remained out.

*   *   *

How to get into history
without getting out of it?

*   *   *

Even when walking on a straight path,
we get over exhausted searching for its end.

*   *   *

After succeeding in penetrating the solar system,
our scandal became galactic.

*   *   *

It accepts in the zone of its disability
that which it rejects in the zone of its consciousness.

*   *   *

To us, faith is like the theory of conspiracy,
we adopt it with folded arms.

*   *   *

Thought …!
A holed vessel that holds attempts for harmony in the
contradictions of the consciousness.

*   *   *

The most exciting thing in playing chess
is the absence of moral deterrent when killing.

* * *

So long as heart is our term of reference,
melancholy is our world.

* * *

Fear has succeeded in containing every idea
it had created to have control on it.

* * *

The most veiling moments
are when we clothe a scandal in a scandal.

*　　*　　*

We dive deep into the depth,
to get onto the surface on the other side.

*　　*　　*

We go along a straight line until the circle is complete.
What a straight line!

*　　*　　*

Their genius waned, attempting
to find new ways to triumph, so they remained like us.

*   *   *

It is enough for feebleness in the old age what convictions it
produces; we don't have to count much on them.

*   *   *

The logic of craziness has always been stronger
than the logic that had created it.

*   *   *

He stood alone on the edge of the memory,
thinking it over to throw himself out.

*   *   *

We defend the things we fear,
those we understand need no defense.

*   *   *

Minor sacrifices are never memorized
so long as major ones are.

*   *   *

The black king finds himself defending.
What a black king daring to defend!

*   *   *

One shouldn't reach a peak
if not well prepared for collapsing.

*   *   *

Who has given the king on the chessboard
the right to sacrifice all his pieces?

*   *   *

One may mean all that one says,
but can one say all that one means?

*   *   *

We are most capable of debating
illogical-based things in a logical manner.

*   *   *

The white pawn shakes hands with the black one,
shockingly to wonder after a while:
"Why did I kill him?"

*   *   *

We are confused how to prove
we are intelligent.

*   *   *

He who wants to kill death
never seeks refuge in the tunnels of life.

*   *   *

When I liberated myself from hope,
I started to breathe.

*   *   *

The most beautiful moments …!
Those during which we realize we live.

*   *   *

A philosopher …!
He who generalizes his personal anxiety.

*   *   *

Looking for solutions
doesn't mean there is a problem.

*   *   *

What might one taste in a life
that entirely tastes worrisome?

*   *   *

Comparing ourselves with whom we think better
causes grief, with whom we think worse causes pity. What a
misery!

*   *   *

A postulate imposes itself,
we don't impose it.

*   *   *

Perhaps because we don't understand history,
it finds itself obliged to repeat itself.

*   *   *

We accept our existence from one position,
but deal with it from another.

*   *   *

The more the flame of life dies out,
the more the hereafter fire flares up.

*   *   *

What to do
when faith can't bind us to act according to its content?

*   *   *

No one ever remembers signing off on
the "Social Contract."

*   *   *

As long as we are alive,
death lives states of abortive suicides.

*   *   *

We enjoy peace …
preparing for war.

*   *   *

The strategic options
are tactical necessities.

*   *   *

Let's finish …
what we haven't started yet.

*   *   *

We fear, if we understand,
to lose our minds.

*   *   *

If the idea is fortified,
I wonder from where to get into it.

*   *   *

We count on the gap of mind inertia
to prove and understand the rational side.

*   *   *

On the chessboard,
even the draw is driven by one of the two parties.

*   *   *

How could he who is part of a conflict,
know the concept of right?

*   *   *

The ideas are like the means of transportation;
they transport us, we don't.

*   *   *

_ Baha Burhan_

One's homeland is one's needs;
one's alienation is one's desire.

*　*　*

Too shy, the king blushed,
after he had sacrificed the queen.

*　*　*

The wider Man's horizon is,
the narrower his world gets.

*　*　*

When unable to answer,
we evaluate the question.

*   *   *

Getting rid of the idea of coercive belonging
liberates the mind.

*   *   *

The dead ones
outnumber the mourners.

*   *   *

Our ignorance gathers us
in pretending that we know.

*   *   *

We wake up to the ugliest of nightmares;
I wonder how we can sleep afterward.

*   *   *

The amount of fear exceeded our ability,
to concede its role.

*   *   *

We want to fill the glass,
while our eyes are on the vessel.

*   *   *

We are awarded blessings,
we did nothing to deserve.

*   *   *

Craziness …!
That zone which comforts us when we are disabled.

*   *   *

Raison d'être and its purpose are the two shelters
that fit our consciousness.

* * *

When we want to extinguish the sun,
we close our eyes.

* * *

We enwrap our certainty
with our doubts.

* * *

The yards of alienation got filled up;
finding himself no room, he returned.

* * *

Covering each other,
is a scandal to us all.

* * *

They always guide us to a way
we could never go along.

* * *

Is the first action,
a reaction?

*   *   *

As if we were looking for something,
to dampen water.

*   *   *

Accepting the truth
is more difficult than discovering it.

*   *   *

Being on the other side,
he is a foe.

*   *   *

Is it an insult to live
on some hope?

*   *   *

To live,
we don't have to kill death.

*   *   *

While inside the pot,
we insist upon lifting it.

*   *   *

Contentment …!
A veiled depression.

*   *   *

What if the black king
stands still?

*   *   *

We attempt not to triumph,
to avoid collapsing afterward.

*   *   *

One's freedom and value are
the two shadows of one's tragedy.

*   *   *

The more confessional we are to our sins,
the more virtuous we get.

*   *   *

He remembered that laws don't allow him to take
his pawn to survive, so he sacrificed all his pieces.
What a king's memory that keeps observing laws.

*　*　*

Right …!
What we can have.

*　*　*

The innocent are
the fuel of the sin.

*　*　*

We have lifted faith so high that
we are no longer able to see it.

*   *   *

While inside a tornado,
we want to specify our stance toward it.

*   *   *

What else, other than faith, to resort to
in order to do whatever we want?

*   *   *

To avoid falling in the trap
we've spent our lifetime therein.

*　*　*

Hope then excuses then excuses, and afterward hope;
that whole situation turns later into a pressure that can't be
tolerated. Therefore, our one and only hope
grows to be giving up hope.

*　*　*

The more we drink wine,
the more we deny we are drunken.

*　*　*

Craziness was most successful
in making mind convinced of what it has come to.

*　　*　　*

Just like a butterfly,
round the light we turn,
coming closer we burn,
keeping off we get lost in darkness.

*　　*　　*

His victory was real.
Therefore, he uttered no word.

*　　*　　*

It is in vain.
As long as protecting the "I" is main.

*   *   *

What might one write on a page
whose margin is even wider?

*   *   *

Although the ideas smell antique,
we don't smell them.

*   *   *

Is it possible for one of the two kings to win,
while the other one is still not a loser?

*   *   *

We always look for a history,
for us to believe.

*   *   *

When the land is sacred,
where on earth shall we walk?

*   *   *

Baha Burhan

We hear them say easy-to-understand and easy-to-accept
things. However, it is our problem,
we aren't good listeners.

* * *

Although so many had come,
virtuous and holy men, pious apostles and prophets,
but it is just like milling the air.

* * *

The black king spent his entire lifetime wondering:
"Why did the white king attack me?"

* * *

Water dried up,
and the fish never drowned.

*   *   *

The inflexibility of the idea
comes from the flexibility of the word.

*   *   *

Logic has brought us onto
an inconceivable defect.

*   *   *

Castles shall remain eyewitnesses to the grandeur of
a civilization built on remnants of the victims
who had fallen while setting them up.

* * *

What else are we looking forward to losing,
after all those losses?

* * *

We dot the i's and cross the t's
of letters that are not yet written.

* * *

Our hope …!
As large as our ignorance.

*   *   *

Although they have collapsed before our eyes, the walls
remain in our consciousness and unconsciousness.

*   *   *

They want to kill you … having stolen their god.
The God is no one property to be stolen by someone.
You've stolen their god, not *the God*.

*   *   *

To them his logic is craziness,
I wonder what his craziness would be.

*   *   *

We insist upon making circles
hurling stones onto an icy land.

*   *   *

Strings care not for he
who holds the plectrum.

*   *   *

Resurrects heritage,
he who doesn't harvest its contradictions.

*   *   *

Each of us creates our own sky,
as the thick clouds veil the sky off our eyes.

*   *   *

As we get more enchanted with our tragedy,
the more eloquent we become in expressing it.

*   *   *

Baha Burhan

The most familiar thing that brings us together
is our allegation, and the strangest thing
that brings us apart is our reality.

* * *

All the words in all the books could never prevent the white
king from issuing a "war declaration" decree.

* * *

From one source of light,
to one thing, we made more than one shadow.

* * *

Man's freedom lies in what he achieves,
his thralldom in keeping thinking.

*   *   *

The two kings continue to be kings,
until the chessboard changes.

*   *   *

In order not to expose us in what we succumb to,
we cover them in what they do.

*   *   *

Baha Burhan

When living between the limits of doubt
and the certainty of fear, we create a thought
that fits in to the genius of our allegations.

*   *   *

As long as we can see,
why do we look?

*   *   *

Despite our disclosure and the collapse of all the protecting
walls, we differ on the details of the place.

*   *   *

When the idea removes but a little fear,
it becomes a burden.

*   *   *

After going conscious,
man cuts short all the ages in his own.

*   *   *

We conceal our fears lest the dark secrets
behind our ignorance should be disclosed.

*   *   *

Our seclusion tightens its grip in us,
unable to perceive our new status,
we get enraptured by the sound
of our ideas clashing together.

*   *   *

Moral …!
To accept the ugliness we do.

*   *   *

The highest degrees of consciousness
are when we face what we aren't prepared for.

*   *   *

The amount of the concessions we have
gone beyond our ability to justify.

*   *   *

As if conflict were an inevitable result
to a justificatory thought, which neglects
our humanity and glorifies our existence.

*   *   *

How could a thought counting on contradictions it brings
forth to live on act as our term of reference
and arbitrator over our life experience?

*   *   *

The step forward narrows,
the way back widens.

*   *   *

We persist on protecting an idea
until it loses its ability to protect us.

*   *   *

Does self-purity
cover the sins of the thought?

*   *   *